YOUR KNOWLEDGE HAS VALUE

Bibliographic information published by the German National Library:

The German National Library lists this publication in the National Bibliography; detailed bibliographic data are available on the Internet at http://dnb.dnb.de .

Imprint:

Copyright © 2015 GRIN Verlag, Open Publishing GmbH
Print and binding: Books on Demand GmbH, Norderstedt Germany
ISBN: 978-3-668-07711-9

This book at GRIN:

http://www.grin.com/en/e-book/306805/critical-review-on-different-types-of-plumes-and-jets

Muhammed Ernur Akiner

Critical review on different types of plumes and jets

Reviewing Cipollina (2005) and Pantokratoras (2003)

GRIN Publishing

GRIN - Your knowledge has value

Since its foundation in 1998, GRIN has specialized in publishing academic texts by students, college teachers and other academics as e-book and printed book. The website www.grin.com is an ideal platform for presenting term papers, final papers, scientific essays, dissertations and specialist books.

Visit us on the internet:

http://www.grin.com/

http://www.facebook.com/grincom

http://www.twitter.com/grin_com

Critical reviews on different types of plumes and jets

Muhammed Ernur AKINER[*, 1]

[1]Akdeniz University, Vocational School of Technical Sciences, Campus, Antalya, Turkey

Summary

Two papers are critically reviewed in this study. These papers are related with the different types of plumes and jets:

Critical review of Bench-Scale Investigation of Inclined Dense Jets": This paper has been written by Cipollina and others (2005) and

Critical review of "Vertical Penetration of Double-Diffusive Water Plumes Discharged Vertically Downward": This paper has been written by Pantokratoras (2003).

All figures in this paper are taken from the aforementioned reviewed articles.

The main goal is to provide new experimental information on the behavior of dense jets issuing from nozzles variously inclined on the horizontal plane (see Fig. 1). Also, to develop suitable Froude number equation for double diffusive plumes, in which discharge temperature is greater than that of the ambient water whereas the discharge salinity is smaller than that of the ambient sea water. Another objective is to prove the Turner`s Equation (Pantokratoras 2003) is unsuitable for double diffusive plumes and to develop this equation.

Most of the investigations on dense jet diffusion dealt with jets issuing vertically in the environment, despite the fact that it has been long known that inclined dense jets result in higher values of dilution.

The water temperature in the tank (1.5 m long, 0.45 m wide, filled with water up to 0.60 m above the bottom) was in the range 18–20° C, $v = 10^{-6}$ m^2/s. The solution employed to feed the jets was colored and prepared by dissolving NaCl in tap water in a suitable lab-scale rectangular batch storage tank. Three different jet densities were tested: 1,055, 1,098, and 1,179 kg/m^3. Brass nozzles have four different diameters (d_0) (1.12, 2, 3, and 4 mm). The initial discharge Reynolds numbers ranged from 2,500 to 10,400, depending on nozzle size and jet features, and therefore flow at the nozzle outlet was always turbulent.

Keywords: Dilution, Froude number, inclined jets, nozzle, plumes, turbulent.

The Distance of the Jet Impact Point from the Origin (X_i in meters): It is an important design parameter for an underwater diffuser as when designing the diffuser it has often to be decided whether and where sea floor protection against erosion is to be provided.

$$F = \frac{u_0}{\sqrt{[(\rho_0 - \rho_a)/\rho_0] \cdot g \cdot d_0}} \tag{1}$$

F is densimetric Froude number, (—), ρ_a= density of ambient water (kg/m3), ρ_0 = density of jet at its source (kg/m3), u_0 = velocity of issuing jet=$Q/(\Pi \times d_0^2/4)$ (m/s), g =gravity constant (m/s^2) and Q = jet volumetric flow rate (m3/s) in (Eq. (1)); Froude number has a simple proportionality with X_i; ($X_i/d_0 = k_i \times F$). k_i value was obtained 2.25 for 60° inclined jets. k_i ,k_z ,k_x ,k_y = coefficients of proportionality between normalized X_i , Z, X, Y and F(−)

Maximum Rise Level (Z in meters): Simple proportionality is found again between Maximum Rise Level (Z in meters) and Froude number ($Z/d_0 = k_z \times F$), with proportionality coefficients k_z of 1.08, 1.61, and 2.32 for jet initial inclinations of 30, 45, and 60°, respectively.

Centerline Maximum Coordinates (X and Y in meters): X and Y are proportional to the Froude number over the whole investigated range ($X/d_0 = k_x \times F$, Y /d$_0$ =$k_y \times F$) with k_x values of 1.95, 1.80, 1.42, and k_y values of 0.79, 1.17, 1.77 for θ_0=30, 45, and 60°, respectively.

Viscosity effect: Jets characterized by two modified values of viscosity (1.77 and 2.97×10^{-3} Pa s). In Fig. 2, the Z values obtained with the modified viscosity jets are compared with each other as well as with data obtained with unmodified viscosity jets (characterized by viscosities ranging from 10^{-3} to 1.5 × 10^{-3} Pa s, depending on salt concentration, i.e., on jet density). Observation of Fig. 2 shows that there is no significant effect of viscosity on the behavior of dense jets. Notably, this is consistent with the assumption of results independent of Reynolds number ($Re = (u_0 \times d_0) \div v$).

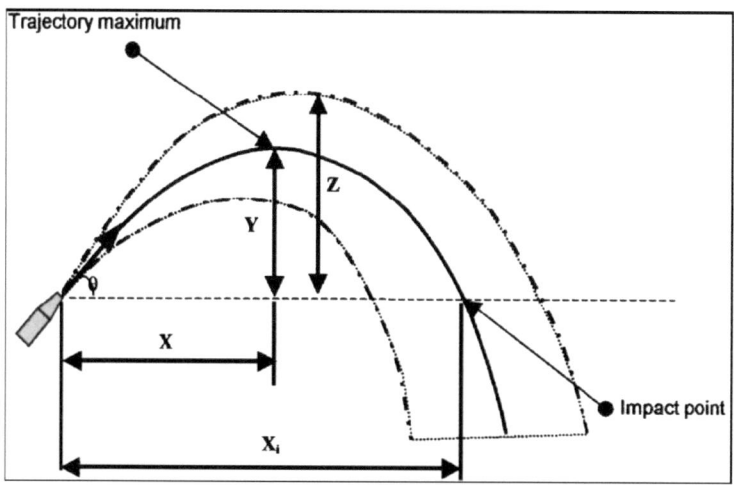

Figure 1: Jet geometrical parameters.

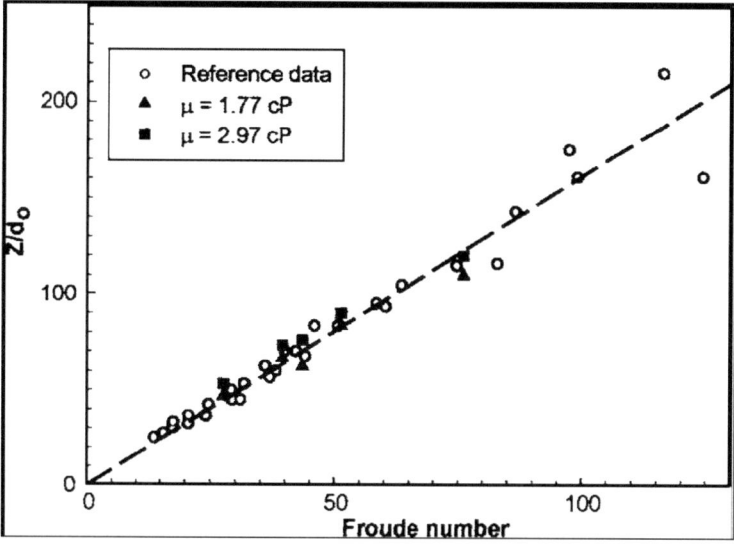

Figure 2: Effect of jet viscosity on max. rise level.

This research is on negatively buoyant jets, where the jet fluid has higher density than the ambient fluid and sinks to the floor. We told mostly about horizontal or vertical positively buoyant jets in the lecture instead of inclined dense jets. Hence, this paper provides a useful contribution to literature.

3

Recommendation: A larger tank would be used for less constraint on the range of parameters such as the nozzle diameter, inclination angle and flow rate.

Critical review of "Vertical Penetration of Double-Diffusive Water Plumes Discharged Vertically Downward": This paper has been written by Pantokratoras (2003). The title of this paper is (see Fig. 3). A discharge with no buoyancy is referred to as a *"nonbuoyant jet"* or *"pure jet"*. A release of buoyancy only (no initial momentum) is called a *"pure plume"*. A discharge with both momentum and buoyancy is call a *"buoyant jet"* or *"forced plume"*. Positively buoyant flows are defined where the buoyancy force acts vertically upwards against the gravity force; negative buoyancy is defined as acting downwards in the direction of the gravity force (Otranto 2004). In this study buoyant jet in other words forced plume is dealt with.

The main goal: To develop suitable Froude number equation for double diffusive plumes, in which discharge temperature is greater than that of the ambient water whereas the discharge salinity is smaller than that of the ambient sea water. Another objective is to prove the Turner's Equation (Pantokratoras 2003) is unsuitable for double diffusive plumes and to develop this equation.

Turner's Equation: Turner developed the following equation for vertical penetration:

$$\frac{Y_m}{D} = c F_o \qquad (2))$$

Where Y_m=terminal rise height; D=jet exit diameter; c=constant; and F_o=initial densimetric Froude number.

Initial Densimetric Froude Number:

$$F_o = \frac{u_o}{\sqrt{gD \dfrac{\rho_a - \rho_o}{\rho_o}}} \qquad (3)$$

In this Froude number u_o and ρ_o=jet exit velocity and density and ρ_a=ambient density. The constant c takes the value of 1.74 according to Turner's measurements.

Pantokratoras (1999) showed that this densimetric Froude number is unsuitable for heated water jets and must be replaced by the effective Froude number.

Effective Froude number for heated water jets:

4

$$F_a = \frac{u_o}{\sqrt{gD\alpha(T_a)(T_o - T_a)}} \qquad (4)$$

Where T_o and T_a are initial (jet exit) and ambient temperatures (°C) and $\alpha\,(T_a)$ =thermal expansion coefficient of water taken at ambient temperature. This finding concerns pure water jets. However, in most discharges from power, manufacturing, and wastewater treatment plants into the sea, there is both a temperature and salinity difference between the discharge and the ambient water. In this case, we have thermosolutal or double-diffusive plumes with two buoyancy components (heat and salt) which both oppose the downward flow.

Eq. (2) including the effective Froude number is not valid in the temperature region $4 <$ $T_a < 10°C$ where the water density–temperature relationship becomes strongly nonlinear.

Maximum densities appear also in saline water.

Eight equations are written for an inclined jet (Pantokratoras 2003).

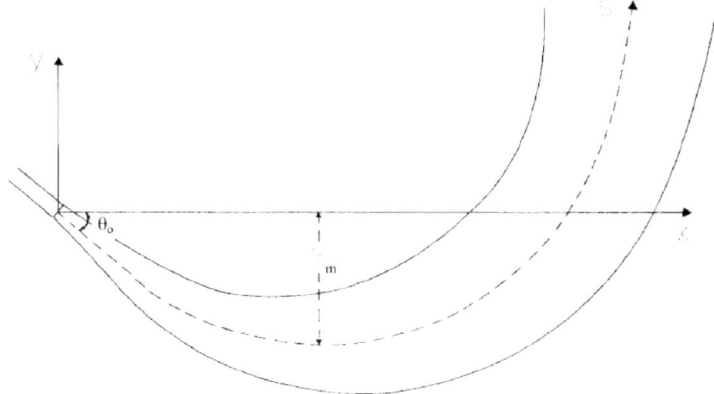

Figure 3: Schematic Diagram of Inclined Buoyant Jet Discharged Downwards.

$$\frac{du(s)}{ds} = \frac{2g\lambda^2}{u(s)}\frac{\rho_a - \rho(s)}{\rho_o}\sin\theta - \frac{2u(s)\alpha_e}{b} \qquad (5)$$

$$\frac{db}{ds} = 2\alpha_e - \frac{b}{u(s)^2}g\lambda^2\frac{\rho_a - \rho(s)}{\rho_o}\sin\theta \tag{6}$$

$$\frac{d\theta}{ds} = \frac{2g\lambda^2}{u(s)^2}\frac{\rho_a - \rho(s)}{\rho_o}\cos\theta \tag{7}$$

$$\frac{d(T(s) - T_a)}{ds} = -\frac{2\alpha_e}{b}(T(s) - T_a) \tag{8}$$

$$\frac{d(S(s) - S_a)}{ds} = -\frac{2\alpha_e}{b}(S(s) - S_a) \tag{9}$$

$$\frac{dx}{ds} = \cos\theta \tag{10}$$

$$\left.\begin{array}{c}\\ \\ \\ \\ \end{array}\right\} \text{Geometric Properties}$$

$$\frac{dy}{ds} = \sin\theta \tag{11}$$

$$\rho(s) = f(T(s), S(s)) \tag{12}$$

Practical salinity (at atmospheric pressure) (Tomczak 2000):

$$S = 0.0080 - 0.1692\ K^{1/2} + 25.3853\ K + 14.0941\ K^{3/2} - 7.0261\ K^2 + 2.7081\ K^{5/2} \tag{13}$$

Centerline density ρ(s) (according to International Equation of State for Seawater):

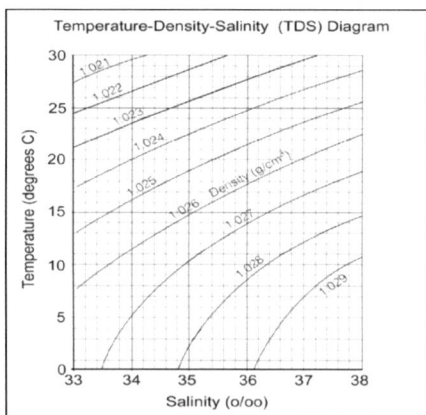

Figure 4: Temperature-Density-Salinity (TDS) Diagram (Huntley 2005).

The equation of state for water: It's given by the following equation (Pantokratoras 1999):

$$\rho = 1 + 3.3 \times 10^{-8} T^3 - 7.4 \times 10^{-6} T^2 + 5.1 \times 10^{-5} T - 9.5 \times 10^{-5} \tag{14}$$

The entrainment coefficient α_e is given by the following equation (Pantokratoras 2003):

$$\alpha_e = 0.0535 - (0.0535 - 0.0833)(R/R_p)^2 \tag{15}$$

Where $R_p = 0.557$ (plume Richardson number) and R is the local Richardson number given by

$$R = \left(\frac{4\sqrt{2}\pi\lambda^2}{1+\lambda^2} \frac{gb \frac{\rho_a - \rho(s)}{\rho_o}}{u(s)^2} \right)^{1/2} = \left(\frac{4\sqrt{2}\pi\lambda^2}{1+\lambda^2} \right)^{1/2} \frac{1}{F_L} \tag{16}$$

In Eq. (16), F_L = the local Froude defined as

$$F_L = \frac{u(s)}{\sqrt{g \frac{\rho_a - \rho(s)}{\rho_o} b}} \tag{17}$$

The parameter λ, which is the spreading ratio between the temperature and velocity profile, takes the value of 1.16 according to Fan and Brooks (1969). The entrainment coefficient:

$$\alpha_e = 0.0535 + 0.5524/F_L^2 \tag{18}$$

There are eight unknowns: (1) centerline velocity u(s); (2) centerline temperature T(s) (°C); (3) centerline salinity S(s); (4) 1/e jet half-width of velocity profile b; (5) angle of inclination θ; (6) and (7) the x and y coordinates of the jet axis; and (8) centerline density ρ(s). The flow establishment zone is taken 6.2D long (xo = 6.2D cos θ_o and yo= 6.2D sin θ_o) according to experimental data by Albertson et al. (1950) (Pantokratoras 2003). Boundary conditions:

u(s) = u(0)

b = D/$\sqrt{2}$

$\theta = \theta_o$

The ratio $(T(s)-T_a)/(T_o-T_a)$ takes the value of 0.70 and $(S(s)-S_a)/(S_o-S_a) = 0.70$.

Effective Froude number for Double-diffusive / thermosolutal plumes:

$$F_a = \frac{u_o}{\sqrt{gD\alpha(T_a)(T_o - T_a) + gD\beta(S_a)(S_a - S_o)}} \tag{19}$$

Where T_o and T_a=initial and ambient temperatures (°C); S_o and S_a are initial and ambient salinities; and $\beta(S_a)$=saline expansion coefficient of water taken at ambient salinity. The thermal and saline expansion coefficients are defined as follows (Pantokratoras 2003)

$$\alpha(T) = -\frac{1}{\rho}\left(\frac{\partial \rho}{\partial T}\right)_{s,p} \tag{20}$$

$$\beta(S) = -\frac{1}{\rho}\left(\frac{\partial \rho}{\partial S}\right)_{T,p} \tag{21}$$

e.g.: for temperature 10 °C, salinity 30 ppt, 100 dbar pressure, alpha $(°C^{-1})$=1.586×10^{-4}, beta (ppt^{-1})= 7.609×10^{-4} (Gill, A. E. 1982).

The nondimensional distance Y_m /D has been calculated experimentally for a water jet discharged vertically downward with the following conditions: u_o=80 cm/s, D=1 cm, T_o=40°C, T_a=10°C, and S_o=0 ppt. The ambient salinity took the values 0, 5, 10, 20, 30, and 40 ppt. From Table 1 it is seen that the values of the constant c which correspond to the effective Froude number (Table 1-last col.) are close to 1.74. Hence, Turner's equation is valid also for double-diffusive plumes if effective Froude number is used, instead of the densimetric Froude number.

Vertical penetration for Double-diffusive / thermosolutal plumes:

$$\frac{Y_m}{D} = c\mathbf{F}_a \tag{22}$$

Table 1. Values of Coefficient c for a Double-Diffusive Plume for Different Ambient Salinities

S_a	Y_m D	F_o	F_a	c for F_o	c for F_a
0	79.9	29.71	49.60	2.71	1.68
5	51.4	23.97	30.73	2.14	1.70
10	41.2	20.74	24.24	1.99	1.71
20	31.8	16.95	18.35	1.88	1.73
30	27.0	14.71	15.39	1.84	1.75
40	23.9	13.19	13.52	1.81	1.77

In the temperature range of 4< T_a < 10°C distance Ym /D has been calculated for a wide range of effective Froude numbers (10–500). From Fig. 5, it is seen that, at low ambient temperatures, the coefficient c is a function of both the ambient temperature and effective Froude number.

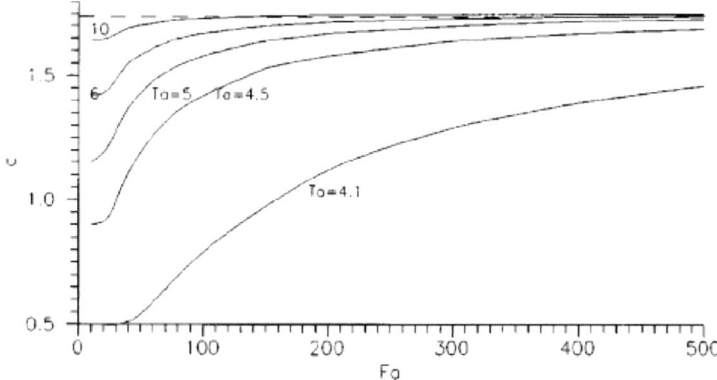

Figure 5: Variation of constant c with effective Froude number and ambient temperature for a vertical fresh water jet discharged downward. The horizontal dashed line corresponds to $c=1.74$.

In this paper both experimental and numerical methods are used simultaneously to achieve the objective. The research is on positively buoyant plumes, where plume density is lower. In the lecture we told about ordinary densimetric Froude number equation. However according to results of this paper, for the extreme cases (such as thermosolutal plumes), densimetric Froude number equation is not suitable and has to be improved in accordance with the flow types and conditions. This paper provides a useful contribution to literature by revealing the unsuitability of densimetric Froude number for double diffusive plumes.

Recommendations for future study

Future study can be implemented on multiport diffusers which are a linear structure consisting of many more or less closely spaced ports or nozzles which inject a series of turbulent jets at high velocity into the ambient receiving water body. Additionally boundary interaction can be investigated which separates near-field (where there is a mixing zone presents, which is the region in which the initial dilution of a discharge occurs) from far-field mixing processes. End of the buoyant jet phase and transition to passive diffusion can be showed. Maybe a new study combines these two papers generates better results.

Future study may be done on more complicated flow pattern such as buoyant jets, which combines jets and plumes to form unique flow characteristics. For instance if the distance from

9

the source (z-defined as "s" by Pantokratoras 2003) is much greater than l_M ($z >> l_M$), then the flow will resemble a plume, properties are dominated by buoyancy flux. If $z << l_M$, the flow will be largely influenced by momentum and initial conditions, thus being jet-like (Otranto 2004).

Momentum length scale is

$$l_M = M^{3/4}/B^{1/2} \qquad (23)$$

or,

$$z/l_M = B^{1/2} \times z / M^{3/4} \qquad (24)$$

If B ↑ then l_M ↓ (Plume like)
If M ↑ then l_M ↑ (Jet like)

Conclusions

New experimental information on the behavior of dense jets issuing from nozzles variously inclined on the horizontal plane was investigated. Additionally, a new effective Froude number is introduced for double-diffusive/thermosolutal plumes. Both papers are quite successful and available for improvement for future studies.

References

Cipollina A., Brucato A., Grisafi F., and Nicosia S. (2005). ASCE Journal of Hydraulic Engineering, Vol. 131, No. 11, pp. 1017-1022.

Fan, L. N., and Brooks, N. H. (1969). ''Numerical solutions of turbulent buoyant jet problems.'' Rep. No. KH-R-18, W. M. Keck Laboratory of Hydraulics and Water Resources, California Institute of Technology, Pasadena, Calif.

Gill, A. E., (1982). Properties of water (and seawater), using the UNESCO equation of state. Atmosphere-ocean dynamics. Academic Press, New York, USA.

Huntley, Anthony C. (2005). Homepage, Saddleback University, California, USA. http://www.saddleback.edu/faculty/thuntley/ms20labs/SEAWATER%20DENSITY.pdf

Otranto, Fabio (2004). Laboratory Modeling of Sea-brine discharges. Thesis Submitted in partial fulfillment of the requirements for the degree of Bachelor of Engineering (Environmental) with honors, The University of Western Australia, Australia.

Pantokratoras, A. (1999). ''Vertical penetration of inclined heated water jets discharged downward.'' J. Environ. Eng., 125(4), 389–393.

Pantokratoras (2003). Vertical penetration of double-diffussive water plumes discharged vertically downwards, ASCE Journal of Hydraulic Engineering, Vol. 129, No. 7., pp. 541-545.

Tomczak, M. (2000). Homepage, Flinders University, Adelaide, Australia. http://www.es.flinders.edu.au/~mattom/IntroOc/notes/lecture03.html

YOUR KNOWLEDGE HAS VALUE